SO NOW YOU KNOW

The battle of a teenage girl fighting her eating disorders in silence

Darah Echevarría

ATHENA PRESS
LONDON

SO NOW YOU KNOW
The battle of a teenage girl fighting her eating disorders in silence
Copyright © Darah Echevarría 2004

All Rights Reserved

No part of this book may be reproduced in any form
by photocopying or by any electronic or mechanical means,
including information storage and retrieval systems,
without permission in writing from both the copyright
owner and the publisher of this book.

ISBN 1 84401 280 8

First Published 2004 by
ATHENA PRESS
Queen's House, 2 Holly Road
Twickenham TW1 4EG
United Kingdom

Printed for Athena Press

SO NOW YOU KNOW

*To my unborn child,
Vincent, the love of my life,
and my best friend and mother, Cecilia*

Before We Start

BEFORE I START WRITING THIS BOOK, I WANT TO share a few thoughts with you, the reader. Whether you are the one who is suffering from an eating disorder or you are reading this because you have a child with an eating disorder, or merely out of interest, it will mean a lot to you.

I suffered from both bulimia and anorexia for nine years (considering I am eighteen, that is half of my life!), in secret most of the time. When practically all you can remember is obsessing over your weight, starving yourself and counting calories, we are no longer talking about a 'phase' that you need to change, but your *life*!

I am no physician, nor can I place a Ph.D. after my name, but I know what it is to live in the hell on earth all people with an eating disorder experience. How every day you promise yourself that you will break out of it and how you feel like such a failure when at the end of the day you did not come through. *You can!* I secretly went to my high school psychiatrist who told me I would never ever beat this problem alone – and I did. Remember, you are so much stronger than you know. You alone have this all in control.

I got so fed up of reading books on eating disorders by physicians who write about these problems from such an objective and emotionless point of view, that I decided to grab my favourite pen and get to work. My mission is to stop this problem as much as I can. If I can save but one girl or boy, then my work is done. If I can only reach one of you out there and make you realise that you are not alone and that this is something you can conquer, this was worth all the time and effort.

It is not as if I am trying to sound like some guru, yelling 'YOU CAN, YOU CAN!' hysterically, I just know that you can overcome it, because of the simple fact that I did. At one time, I even reached a point in my life where I gave up the fight. I actually said to myself that bulimia had become a part of me and that I would have to learn to live with it. Recognise this? Believe me, there will be many, many other parts in this book which will make you think, 'So, I am not the only one who feels, thinks and experiences that?'

Eating disorders should get more attention in our society. Bulimia and anorexia are killing too many of us *and it has to end!*

Many people say that the media is to blame for this problem; I guess it does have a great deal to do with it. Now it is the media's turn to do something in return to help improve the present situation. Mass attention should also be used for the good: normal, healthy bodies on TV, no more using 80-pound girls as symbols of beauty! Nice clothes in all sizes! (At least in Europe we need this) – it can be done! The greatest beauty there is, is health. We all know that famous people, especially pop stars and actors, are looked up to in society– then please tell me what good we get from placing unrealistic 'role models' on the TV screen?

What is the message that we are giving young girls and teenagers? Basically, we are saying that if they want to be beautiful (and every girl does) they have to weigh twenty pounds under their normal weight. Celebrities should use their fame for the good and if they choose to be famous then they must acknowledge that their appearance will be of great influence to many people. I am not saying that there is something wrong with being thin – of course not; that is, if you are built that way. My concern lies with those, and especially women, who go against everything Mother Nature gave them in order to resemble a magazine cover.

I wish you, as the person with the eating disorder as well as the family member or friend, luck and strength in order to overcome this problem. But remember this problem is not everlasting and definitely has a solution, which rests inside of you.

Good luck!

Darah Echevarría

One

I REMEMBER EXACTLY HOW I STARTED BECOMING bulimic. One night (when I was nine), we were having spaghetti and I felt really full, so I went to the toilet and I regurgitated the food. I never had to put my finger down my throat to provoke vomit or anything. It was so easy that I thought, *Wow, this must be some kind of blessing! I can eat all I want without gaining any weight!* I believed that I was truly blessed.

Now you are thinking, *What is a nine-year-old worrying about her weight for?* Believe me, I did. To be honest I cannot remember a time when my weight was not an obsession to me. It has always occupied my thoughts. But for you to understand why, I need to go even further back in time. Four years earlier, to be exact.

When I was five years old my grandmother came from Mexico to live with us. Both my parents worked outside the house during the day and because my grandmother had not been working for a long time in Mexico, my mother suggested she come and stay with us, so that my sister and I did not need to go to day care. When I was five, I was thin – no, wait, I was skinny! To be honest I was a bit too skinny, but nevertheless, I was healthy. My grandmother came with the Mexican mentality from two centuries ago, which was that children needed to be fat in order to be healthy and, well, considering I was thin, she concluded I was unhealthy. Grandma found a new mission in her life, which was to 'pork Darah up'!

Don't get me wrong – I enjoyed that phase. My mother had fed my sister and I only healthy things: fruits, vegetables, whole wheat bread, etc. So when Granny came with candy, stacks of pancakes with butter and syrup, fried potato pancakes, apple pie and other forbidden stuff, my sister and I (but specially myself) went mad with hunger! I could not believe my luck, my home had become a McDonald's restaurant and I was customer of the year! Being 'customer of the year' did not come without a price: I started gaining weight.

When you are that young, you don't notice immediately when you gain weight. The things I would pick up were the fights between my mother and grandmother about what she was feeding us and specially me, because I was the one who was clearly becoming overweight. What made me acknowledge this 'new-found problem' were the comments at school. It was almost as if I started getting bullied from one day to the next, without any transition – from not ever having been teased to being the class's 'fat girl'. The girl boys would tease other boys with by saying 'Darah is your girlfriend' by means of insult. Every time we had a project on animals the guaranteed comments would come about how I resembled the fat animals, such as the elephants, pigs, cows, etc. Understand that the insults could not be so sophisticated – we are talking about elementary school here.

Still, every comment was like a knife to the heart and the way I saw myself kept getting worse and worse.

When I was about ten (already bulimic, but didn't know it) I changed schools, hoping that the last two years of elementary could leave some good memories behind, but boy was I wrong. Instead of being teased by a group of children, I now had the whole damn class making fun of me! They would literally chant insults at me and laugh at me together. It scared me how such a beautiful thing as laughter could sound so terrifying and satanic. Every single day I would walk to school hoping that nothing would trigger insults or mockery; sadly enough, almost every single day would, in that sense, be a disappointment. A great day to me would be a day that I was unnoticed. A wish to be popular? Forget it! I wanted to be invisible, I didn't even want friends. I *wanted to be left alone.* By now, you understand, my self-esteem was on the floor. Who was the ugliest? I was. Who was the fattest? I was. Who would never get married? Me.

I was brainwashed to think that I was robbing others of air and that if I was allowed to be somewhere I should keep the lowest profile possible. This to me was extremely hard, because I was never the typical shy kid who would get teased. I was (and still am) very lively, loved jokes and dancing, so taking on that attitude went against everything I was but if that was going to guarantee being left alone, then that was okay with me. I have always had an amazingly close bond with my mother – she is my all! Still, your mother telling you that you are pretty doesn't sound convincing, when five days a week you hear the complete opposite.

I was an early bloomer, so I started noticing boys very early. I always had a crush on someone who never had a crush on me. I calculated that by process of elimination, if nobody acknowledges your existence, the odds are the person you like most probably will not like you. I heard all the insults and humiliations one girl can take. And still, if after all that torture and pain I can today look at myself in the mirror and in life and say that I am happy with who I am, I guess I was stronger than all the other kids all along. Being able to say that, on the other hand, was not something I learned to say overnight.

Back to my story. So I had gone to this new school (also known as the dungeon from hell) which made my old school look like Disneyland. Everyday, I would cry myself to sleep and one night it came to me! The problem, the source of my pain, was the fact that I was overweight. What was the solution? To eat less, but that was so hard. Before this time, I had already been throwing up, but not with losing weight as my main goal but to avoid the discomfort which being full brings. It was like this: 'Oh, I eat too much, let's throw it out.' So eating less was too much of a sacrifice; what was the next option? That's it! Why not throw everything up after eating, so that nothing stays in my stomach and I'll definitely lose weight! That was my solution; it sounded too good to be true and believe me, it was. Not long after I started doing that did my mother find out.

I had left (sorry for the nasty details) some vomit in the toilet and she called me on it. I felt embarrassed and it was weird, because I did not think that I was doing something wrong, but on the other hand, I kept it to myself, so I must have known it wasn't right either. She called me to come to the toilet and asked me what was going on. I told her that my stomach pushed back the food when I ate too much and that I would throw it out. I told her how children at school made fun of my weight and that this was a solution to my problem. My mother held me close and started crying. She sat me down and told me that I had bulimia.

That was the very first time I heard the word. My mother told me how it was a disorder that could kill me, and how my brain and other organs would suffer because of the deprivation of vitamins that my body needed. Now I knew throwing up was bad for me.

After our talk I promised my mother that I would never ever throw up again to try and lose weight. I saw how upset my mother was because of what I did, so I myself believed that the problem stopped there. Little did I know that it was just the beginning.

The problem at school didn't stop that easily. I still didn't conform to what the other children saw as 'normal' so they still teased me. I would get upset, seek comfort in food and after a few times that I did stop myself from throwing up, I gave in. It was easier this way. I loved (and of course still do) my mother and I didn't want to hurt her, so I had to take other measures this time: I had to hide what I was doing more carefully, and so all the lies started. It is incredible how sickeningly resourceful one is with an eating disorder. Not illogical, because the disorder not only becomes your obsession, it becomes your *life*. This doesn't mean you're at ease knowing you have covered your steps; on the contrary, you are constantly nervous that someone might catch you. Every time my mother went to the toilet to brush her hair or do her make-up and she happened to call me, I would freeze – I feared that she had found out. Only people with an eating disorder know this feeling. You feel like a liar, alone and miserable – it is really horrible!

When you finally do lose weight, you feel good for about a second when you are standing on the scale and then you realise that you took the easy road and that you cheated yourself. You never feel good about yourself.

I did lose weight. I lost a lot of weight, but not in a short period of time – I guess that was another reason why I didn't really attract much attention to myself. It is hard for me to remember the exact order of everything, I am talking about nine years of my life. It is so sad to see pictures of myself where I am smiling, knowing the inner war I was facing at that very moment. I would look up websites on eating disorders, sometimes trying to scare myself out of it. For the next day or two I would be all motivated to stop, and I would feel happy, in control and victorious even, but then when I fell back, the drop would be deeper than it was before.

I always felt different from everyone else and I tried not to show it. I am not going to claim that I *wanted* to be different, I hated it! I hated the fact that I looked different, that I liked different things and had a completely different taste in just about everything. I wanted to conform and be like the rest. When you are a teenager it's normal to want to be different and stand out, but we all know that before you hit puberty all you want is to blend in. When I turned ten I had a little party (little, for the simple reason that I had few friends) and in Holland it's a normal thing to watch a movie and eat junk food. Specially because my birthday is December 1st, which means it is pretty cold and so there is little you can do. Anyway, I rented 'Husbands and Wives', which at the time was my absolute favourite movie. I was brought up with Woody Allen movies, Isabel Allende books and jazz music; I really had nothing in common with kids my age.

I was different, and different was weird; in other words, different = bad. I am sociable, don't get me wrong. I love being around people and all, but I was the kid who would participate in the adult conversation downstairs while the kids were playing upstairs. I didn't care for the new Disney movie, I hated cartoons and I did not enjoy things like the circus or the zoo. I wrote poetry from the age of nine and loved theatre, acting and dancing. One of my favourite childhood memories is dancing with my mother to old Motown music from the 70s. But all these things had to happen in secret, because otherwise children would have another reason to tease and dislike me. Around the age of eleven or twelve, you aren't strong enough to say, 'This is who I am, if you like me, fine. If not, too bad.' I became a great actress. I acted the way people expected me to act at school, so that they would leave me alone and at home I could be myself (with my mom, that is).

When I first heard about bulimia I thought, *That is not what I have!* The physician on TV spoke of a disease which was caused by lack of control in your life. I felt that my problem was purely related to my weight. I threw up in order to lose weight, or so I thought. Now I look back and it is clear that at least a great deal of my problem was indeed caused by a lack of control. I couldn't control the way I looked, I couldn't control whether kids at school liked me or not and when I tried to control my happiness by going to another school, it blew up in my face. I felt like I didn't have a say in anything which was going on in my life and that probably caused the bulimia to go on as long as it did, though I don't know for sure. I can go on for days on end analysing what could have caused this problem, but it's no use now. I know you should dig deep inside of yourself and search the real cause behind it all; in my case I know I have more than one reason, but still. I hope that sharing my story and experience will allow you to find some sort of support which will help lift you out of your own private misery (what I believe it is).

An eating disorder isn't a little thing – *it can kill you!* For a young person it is hard to acknowledge this, but even if you are young and look healthy despite all the damage you inflict on your body, you are still hurting yourself. Because of bulimia I have suffered physically and mentally. There are so many side effects that one doesn't recognise as such. Pain in your throat, bad skin, loss of hair, headaches, anaemia, a damaged stomach, shortness of breath, depression, heart palpitations, anxiety attacks, the shakes, and many,

many more are all caused by bulimia. I had tried to fool myself by thinking, *Oh, the fact that I feel weak has nothing to do with the fact that I throw up* and other stuff like that. You feel that as long as you don't acknowledge the problem to yourself, there isn't one.

Two

I FELT LIKE SUCH A LIAR AND A FAILURE, AMONG other things. It was a lose-lose situation and there was no way of escaping. I wasn't honest to anyone around me and worst of all, I was not honest with myself. I could never win, even when I had lost weight (which was initially what I had wanted) I still felt like I had failed. I felt like I did not deserve that satisfaction of standing on the scale and seeing my weight go down because I had not really worked for it. On the streets every overweight person was a constant reminder of how my eating habit should make me look and it would trigger the thought: *at least they are honest, at least they are exposing their weakness.* They had the guts and I did not. I was an over-eater and the worst part is that I didn't even *enjoy* the food.

I firmly believe that you should listen to your body. During all those years of torture I found my body yelling out and begging me to stop my stupid ways. It is such a tricky and unfair game, because you think that you are taking the easy route by throwing up, while you are paying the highest price for what you are doing. You feel like a failure when you can't say no to food and start to eat; you feel like a failure when you are full and then you really feel like a failure when you find yourself throwing up, but the worst part is after. After throwing up, you feel your heart race (sometimes you start shaking), the pressure in your head from forcing the vomit up and most agonising of all, the loneliness you experience at that moment. Earlier, I mentioned that I didn't even enjoy the food – because you don't, you *can't*. Every time I ate, it was as a preparation to throw it up. I'll explain this in further detail.

Every bulimic has favourite 'throw-up foods'. There are certain meals which you can easily regurgitate without anything being left behind in your stomach (that is what you want to achieve). I drank enough fluids so that I would be able to throw up more easily, but I wouldn't drink too much, because then I only succeeded in throwing up the fluids when what I was interested in was getting the solids out. It's sick. I started losing my life; the only things I thought about was my weight and what I had eaten that day.

Once I started eating I had to eat more and more until I was really full, which made it easier for me to throw it up again. I ate the weirdest combinations in order to get full: whole loaves of bread with mayonnaise, pasta with apple sauce, tuna fish with lentils… At one point, it wasn't even about what the food tasted like as long as it filled my stomach enough.

I pray to God for forgiveness for what I have done. I have wasted so much food for nothing! I am blessed to be able to eat whenever I want, when there are millions of people all over the world who fight daily to survive – I am truly ashamed.

The way these disorders totally rule your life is awful. Whenever I tried stopping and curing my disorder, a simple invitation to a BBQ would be enough of an excuse not to pull through. 'Why should I stop now that it is Monday, when on Saturday I know I am going to eat too much at the BBQ?' It was as if food equalled failure. If I were to find myself in a situation where there was going to be food, then I had an excuse not to stop throwing up. It actually never occurred to me that sooner or later I was going to have to face food and a social event where it was going to be served. That's not the only way an eating disorder (in this case, bulimia) rules your life – it messes you up in other ways as well.

Whenever I was visiting a house, hotel, or any place away from my home for that matter, I always needed to check the water pressure in the bathroom. Bad water pressure meant that the toilet wouldn't flush hard enough and that it might clog, so that was something I always needed to check. Another thing was how fast I needed to go to the bathroom after having eaten. I never wanted to wait too long, because I was afraid that I would start metabolising the food. The problem was doing it without being noticed, so I would have to use excuses like 'I think I got my period', or 'Damn, I drank too much water' and run to the bathroom. As a bulimic you constantly need excuses and little tricks, which is so very tiring. You can't be honest, and perpetually need to clean up any traces – you can never rest.

At times when I lost weight, I could never show it off, because it just would not make sense to my mother that I had lost weight after having eaten as much as I had. This meant that I needed to hide it by wearing baggy clothes. Another thing is that I have never really been skinny. People tend to think that someone who suffers from an eating disorder is skinny; this not always the case. I was quite overweight when I started suffering from bulimia; when I really lost weight was around the age of thirteen or fourteen, when my problem went to anorexia.

It was the summer of '98 and I was at home (alone) for six weeks straight. All of my friends at the time had gone to their home country or were just on vacation during that time. I just sat there on the couch watching all the programmes on television till my mom came home. I was annoyed with myself, because each year (during summer) I would tell myself, 'This will be the summer that I lose all the weight that I have always wanted to lose and I will go back to school looking great.' I was never satisfied with how I looked or how much I weighed by the time classes started, which again made me feel like a loser, but that year I told myself that it was going to be different.

I started making schedules for myself of what I was allowed to eat. Under this page (and in the back of this book) you will find some pages of my diary from a few years ago.

★

August 8th 1998

I am so f**king fat!

I hate it! Why can't this damn weight come off? I want to be beautiful for once in my life! Today I am going to start my diet and this time I will pull through,

I need to! I am so sick of not looking the way I want to look. I *have to* follow the schedule below and I will lose 1 kg[1] a day. For f★★k's sake I need to be able to do something right in my life! Or am I too much of a loser to do that as well?

Breakfast
2 apples
100 calories

Lunch
2 apples
100 calories

Dinner
2 apples
100 calories

Total = 300 calories

August 9th, 1998

I lost a kilo! Now I weigh 68 kg,[2] only 18 more to go! I am really tired, though. That doesn't matter, 'cause I have all day to lie around the house anyway. I am scared that my mother might notice. Yesterday I had to lie about what I ate, because she only saw me eating the two apples for dinner. I don't want to worry her. It's not like I am going to do this for the rest of my life; as soon as I reach my goal – 50 kg[3] – I will eat normally again.

---

[1] About 2 lbs.
[2] About 140 lbs.
[3] About 100 lbs.

Three

MY EATING DISORDERS PUSHED ME TO OTHER THINGS as well. I started drinking heavily around thirteen. I noticed that drinking made me feel better.

I need to give you some background information though, before I go on. The Netherlands is different from all the other countries in the world in that almost anything is accessible here to young people. The legal age for drinking beer and wine is sixteen as well for smoking; for hard liquor you need to be eighteen (supposedly). Every young person, though, knows that as long as you don't look like a three-year-old, you can get a shot of tequila (my favourite drink back then) served in any bar. Consequently, I was never refused alcohol.

When I was twelve or thirteen I started going out to clubs with my sister, who is about four years my senior. In The Netherlands, sixteen is an acceptable age to go out at night. But I knew how to use my communicative skills in my favour and persuaded my mom to let me go with her. I was an early bloomer so I looked older than my age, but I was still a twelve-year-old kid. A friend of my sister's invited me for a tequila and I remember thinking that one shot would kill me, but it didn't. I felt great! I wasn't shy anymore, I would talk to guys I liked, would dance to all my favourite songs without having to wait for others to start dancing; I had fun and most importantly, I didn't care about my weight. Drinking was an escape from all the problems I was dealing with, but after a while getting drunk would only remind me of how sad I really was inside. Another thing is that I wouldn't only drink at parties; at a certain point in my life, it was something I did before, during and after school and I was amazing at hiding it! My eating disorders had made me an Oscar-winning actress so when I started drinking heavily it was only one more thing I had to hide.

My capacity to drink started increasing dramatically to the point that at the age of fourteen I out-drank a 25-year-old, six foot five, heavily-built army guy. Back then I thought it was cool and my sister saw me as a little trophy – she was so proud. Now I just think how sad it was. I think it is sad because I now know and acknowledge where that all came from and that it was a place of hurt inside of me that caused me to throw up, deprive myself of food, smoke like a chimney and drink like crazy.

Now I look back and see that it was auto-destruction that was taking place, or, in other words, a slow form of suicide. I don't know how I am here today and able to write about that kind of life as if it took place in another world, because that is exactly how it feels – like a past life. After all that physical and mental damage that I went through I promised God and myself that I would at least make the best out of the situation. I could do something in order to reach others by telling my story, and maybe be of some comfort and help to others who were facing the same kind of situation that I was back then. Again, that is now how I look back and see all of it – as if it all took place in another world and to another person, someone who died because of all the torture and cruelty that she had inflicted on her body.

Around the age of fourteen was when I started getting noticed by boys. I could not believe it; me getting noticed? I had lost a bit of weight, but was still quite pudgy. When I asked my mother about my weight she would always say, '*No estas gorda, estas llenita,*' which means, 'No, you are not fat, you are full figured', which of course sounds a lot better. Like I said before, I was an early bloomer, and so I already had developed breasts and round hips, which attracted older guys, I did not get involved with them or anything, but I did enjoy the attention. First I was filled with disbelief, but later I thought that I would get even more attention if I simply lost more weight.

Now, I not only had bulimia (with the occasional waves of anorexia), I was also an alcoholic chain-smoker before even entering high school. One thing I do have to say is that I never got into drugs, not even soft drugs. This is a huge accomplishment in The Netherlands, believe me. I didn't, not because I was such a 'good girl', but I guess because I was scared that I would truly lose control. I have an addictive personality. I was never the kind to eat one cookie out of the jar and close it; I would eat till I hit the bottom. I believe I was always aware of what I was doing and what was going on inside of me and even though I was destroying myself (and I was) I didn't dare to fall that deep, so that meant there was, somewhere inside of me, a will to live. I wanted to get out of the prison I was in. I was being controlled by my eating disorder, I was controlled by my alcohol problem and I was controlled by the distorted image that I had of myself. I wanted my life back.

One thing I want you to know (if you have an eating disorder) is, don't give up! If you don't get it right the first time, the second or the third does not mean that you never will.

I would try not to throw up after eating, not to drink and not to light a cigarette either – it wasn't easy. I won't tell you that I stopped in one go, no! I really started trying to stop from the age of fifteen and it didn't really work until I was almost eighteen. I am not saying that you can't stop in one go; *you can do anything you want to.* It may sound like a huge cliché and maybe it is, but it is true: you have it in control. You make the choice to go to the toilet or to stay seated at the table, nobody else is forcing you! It is so ironic, because the whole lack of control which causes the problem of bulimia or anorexia is something you already have inside of you. You already have that control you long for and only you decide whether you want to let it out or not. In my opinion, the thing which makes eating disorders seem so impossible to overcome is that people talk about it like you are being possessed by something larger than yourself; you are not. You have the upper hand, don't forget it. As I may have said before, I don't see eating disorders as an illness, I compare them more to addictions.

You cannot 'fall off the wagon' with an illness. An illness is something that suddenly hits you out of the blue; bulimia and anorexia don't fall out of the sky.

People with an eating disorder need to know that you can fight and overcome the problem, that you do have it in control. I am definitely not playing down the problem; on the contrary, it can and will kill you if you don't stop it. All I want people to know is that the problem can be solved, that is all. I am no doctor, I haven't studied cases, but I did have bulimia and anorexia and I know what it is. I overcame it and so can you. In my opinion, the only thing someone needs in order to overcome an eating disorder is the will to live.

I am not stating that kicking your smoking habit can be compared to overcoming an eating disorder, the only thing I want to make clear is how powerful the human mind really is. I smoked for six years (like crazy). I would actually put the little clock on TV to time the minutes between cigarettes. After putting out a cigarette I had to wait two minutes to light the next one. All I heard was people talking on TV and other media about how impossible it was to quit. Imagine when I heard that to quit smoking was almost a guarantee to gain weight! I stalled quitting for a while for that reason.

The day I quit was not planned. I had given my mom a weekend to Paris for her birthday and because she hates cigarette smoke, I promised her that I would not smoke during that weekend. The whole weekend we had so much fun visiting all the tourist attractions that I did not have time to think about smoking, nor did I eat more. After getting back from Paris, I realised that I had not smoked for five days and said to myself, *Why not go for the whole week?* The week became two weeks, those two weeks became a month and so on. This was the impossible thing? This was the habit no one could kick? What I am trying to say is that people tend to underestimate the greatness of will-power.

Doctors know a great deal because they have studied similar cases in the past, but remember, they are not gods. Doctors have made mistakes in the past and they will keep on making mistakes until they have all the answers to all the health problems in this world (and that is still a long way away). So, what they say is not absolute. Remember that cases which are *similar*, but never *identical*, to yours have been studied in the past, but every study was held on a different person and every individual is unique and responds in a unique way to different circumstances. Of course there are many doctors out there who can help you with this problem, or at least can guide you. I was told by a psychiatrist that bulimia was something that I could never ever beat alone. Here I am healthy and bulimia-free, so much for your water-tight theory, Doc! Listen to the advice that helps you; what matters is that it works for you! Whether the magic words are pronounced by a teacher, your neighbour or your best friend is irrelevant; does it help you overcome your inner war? If so, then that is exactly what you need.

Don't get me wrong, there are many great psychologists, psychiatrists and doctors, but in my case the so-called good advice that I had gotten could have killed me, or at least made me believe that I would never have the strength to defeat my problem alone. And that wasn't true. Having faith in yourself can only bring good things for you in life and that is not only the case with eating disorders, but with everything that awaits you in the future.

When it comes down to it, we are all humans and good advice is not guaranteed by a university degree, but is whatever makes you want to change your ways for the better.

Four

I WOULD HAVE TO SAY THAT I WAS AT MY WORST AT the age of fifteen or sixteen. In that time I would even throw up water, all because I was terrified of retaining it and not being able to lose the weight caused by it. In that time I had lost quite a lot of hair and my skin condition was horrible. The smallest pimple would turn into a wound, which could take weeks to heal (and that's not even counting the huge scar it would leave). I felt light-headed most of the time and would describe the feeling to my mother as 'feeling absent'. Of course I would leave out the part that I wasn't keeping any food in.

The nights were the worst. First of all, it would take me hours to get to sleep. I would lie in bed with my heart beating like crazy, not being able to breath and literally begging God to let me make it through the night. I got panic attacks for no reason. I felt an overwhelming fear of something unknown. The times that I promised myself that I was never going to throw up again seem countless. At night, when it is dark, everything seems to be more serious and weightier than during the daytime. During the day all those promises vanished in my mind and those terrible nights seemed like something so very distant, when the only thing between the two was a slight difference of a few hours. I used to dread those lonely and painful nights so much. I think the reason why I feared those nights is that they were moments of confrontation.

During those nights, my body would confront me with all the damage that I had caused it, and that hurt most of all. My heart pounded faster than ever; even in an upright position my lungs wouldn't be able to collect enough oxygen and sweat seemed to come out of each pore in my body.

During the day, when I was around people, I could still fool myself into thinking that I was okay and that I was actually as happy as I pretended to be. When I saw the way people reacted to whom I pretended to be, it worked as a reaffirmation that there was no problem. I thought to myself, *If they believe I am a healthy and happy girl and that is what I exude, then that is what I must be.* I was the self-assured, easy-going girl (probably the last person to suffer from an eating disorder, in the eyes of others). People can become so incredibly resourceful at times, it really is unbelievable.

★

Here is a message for all parents out there: *it is not always your fault.*

Please understand this: that you can be an excellent parent and still have a child with an eating disorder. As a parent, you raise your children with love and try to guide them as much as you can, but you are not with them twenty-four hours a day, nor can you look inside their head. This does not make you a bad parent – it just doesn't make you God! I know no one who has the relationship that I have with my mother. I adore my mother, she is my everything. It wasn't the case that I didn't tell her because we didn't talk. I didn't tell her because I didn't want to give her problems. My sister had always been the one to keep my mother up at night and I refused to put her through the same. I have always had a very clear sense of independence and the motto 'I can do it on my own'. To this day, I hate asking for help and maybe that is why I was stuck in my problem for as long as I was. I used to see asking for help as a sign of weakness. If I was as strong as I thought I was, I could deal with things all alone, right? Wrong! I should have asked for help, I should have told my mother, my doctor or anyone else for that matter. I was so embarrassed to admit that I had been suffering from a problem for so long, one that I couldn't get out of. Why?

Why did I have these unrealistic expectations when it came to myself? Why was it okay for others to seek help and not for me? It's not logical and it wasn't that I was arrogant either, thinking that I was able to take on more than others. I just didn't want to be a burden to anyone, especially not my mother. Now that I am writing this, I think that that was it. I didn't want to cause problems. I preferred to suffer horribly on my own any time rather than cause my mother a sleepless night; *I can handle it*, I thought. I have a very strong maternal instinct, which makes me feel the need to take care and protect those around me, but this went too far. This time I was killing myself, and that is when I realised: what would happen if I did die? Because you can. You don't need to look like a skeleton in order to be in the danger zone. I heard on 'Oprah' that you can have a stroke after only a few days, because of a potassium deficiency.

My need to protect my mother could have had the opposite result – I could have caused her a mother's worst nightmare, which is losing a child. Is that what I wanted to achieve? No, it wasn't! I could have kept my secret watertight and then what? My mother would have lost me due to unknown reasons, and when she finally found out, she could spend the rest of her life blaming herself for my death, thinking that she should have paid more attention to me. This was not going to happen! My love for my mother outweighed the love I had for myself and so this was my motivation. It doesn't matter who or what makes you see the light; what matters is that you do. I don't believe that you can only love others once you love yourself; what I wrote above is a proof of that. Saving myself at the time was not enough of a motivation to stop me, but my mother was. She helped me without knowing, she helped me just by being there and by being the incredible mother that she is. This was to me a daily reminder why I needed to fight my problem... in order to stay alive for her.

There is one memory in particular which has made a greater impact on me than any other memory having to do with bulimia has. This event took place a few days after my seventeenth birthday. I came home from school, wet, because it was raining, and hung my coat up. I went straight to the kitchen after that and started bingeing like crazy. I ate a whole loaf of bread with peanut butter, a can of tomato soup, two packs of stroopwafels (Dutch cookies filled with caramel syrup) and chocolate milk. I would take breaks in between foods, so that I could go to the bathroom and throw up. After throwing up I would have more room in my stomach to keep on eating, and I would. Every time I went to the bathroom I would throw up until my stomach felt as if it was pulling together and was empty. I really do not know why I went on eating, because I had not been enjoying the food for a long while already. The last time that I came back from the bathroom I felt my heart racing and knees shaking violently, so violently that I fell on the floor. Once lying on the floor, I started to cry hysterically. I remember feeling extremely afraid, tired and more than anything, lonely. *How did I end up here?* I remember asking myself.

It is one thing to become ill by accident, another thing to make yourself ill by purposefully depriving your body of any nutrition, by throwing food up or starving yourself.

My mom knew during the first years of my bulimia, but with age comes tricks and I was able to fool people better and better than the year before. I would even criticise thin girls and make statements like 'I'd rather be fat than look like them,' and I would tell everyone that wanted to hear that I was more than happy with my round figure, so people didn't suspect anything! Again, people think that you need to weigh 30 kg in order to have an eating disorder; you don't. I had a normal weight, leaning more towards voluptuous than anything. Whenever anyone asked me whether I had put on weight, I completely panicked.

Physically, I panicked. The blood rushed to my face

and my heart beat like crazy. If there was a piece of paper and something to write with, I anxiously wrote out my ridiculous diet for the next day, which never consisted of more than 500 calories. That was my life.

After waking up I rushed to the bathroom and weighed myself. This determined whether I was going to have a good or a bad day. If I had lost weight I was happy, and if I had put on weight I was sad and sometimes even skipped school. I felt that everyone was able to tell whether I had put on a pound. Staying home meant not being confronted with food and gave me the time to read magazines. I could see the bodies that I was aiming to look like and starve myself during the process. During these 'waves of anorexia' as I called them, I was supposedly trying to fight my bulimia. I actually thought that this was better; I thought I was in control. I wasn't throwing up, so this was a huge improvement, which it wasn't.

During the summer, a few years ago, my mother did finally catch on. She saw that I was constantly weak and forced me to eat food. Before that day I really was convinced that I was doing okay and that I no longer had an eating disorder. Okay, I was eating very little and I was still counting every calorie I ate. I even wondered whether water really didn't have calories or whether doctors had just rounded the few calories up to nothing? Because in that case I was still consuming calories and I had to look out. But I wasn't throwing up; wasn't that what I had always wanted? I remember sitting in front of that plate with my mother next to me saying that she was not moving till I had finished eating everything (and this was only a tuna salad). I was scared. The food scared me – I was actually afraid to eat it. I tried to explain that I had already eaten all my calories for that day. My mother was now even more worried than before and said that she didn't care and that she would check me into a hospital if I kept that up.

This scared me, because I never thought that what I was doing was wrong for me – so wrong that it could ever involve medical care. I ate the salad. I felt better physically, I can't deny. I felt more energetic and was able to be more active, but emotionally I felt as if I had failed. I wanted to throw up again, but I didn't. My mother stayed with me the whole time so that I couldn't get away from her. The whole night I kept on praying that I wouldn't put on the weight again.

During those weeks I did lose quite a lot of weight, but I was constantly weak, couldn't concentrate and despite the fact that it was summer, I was pale. I naturally have brown skin and when you have darker skin you look even sicker when you lose a bit of colour.

There is a huge difference between losing weight in a healthy way by exercising, drinking water and staying away from fatty and sweet foods and starving or throwing up. I didn't keep in contact with my friends anymore and I didn't go out; I started excluding myself from the world and was stuck in my own, the one I had created. I felt so alone. I cannot even start to describe how one feels at that moment; the only thing I know is that the dominating emotion is without a doubt loneliness. It is hard for me to find an exact order to what I felt at what time, because I am talking about so many years and trying to give everything I went through a place in this book.

A few days ago, I was talking to some people at work about eating disorders, when one of the girls told me the most horrifying news. Apparently there are websites which promote eating disorders! I could not (and still cannot) believe this. How can people encourage others to join them in their misery? Maybe the old saying 'misery loves company' has some truth to it. I was completely flabbergasted. In my case it had the opposite effect; anyone I spotted going to the toilet after having eaten worried me terribly. When my sister went to the toilet after eating, I would put my ear to the door just to check whether everything was okay.

Maybe what I am going to say is really terrible, but here it goes. I believe anyone putting tips on a website on how to hide your anorexia or bulimia is helping someone commit suicide. I want to remind you that everything I write in this book is only the way *I* see things, from the perspective of someone who has suffered the same problem as these girls who are adding information to these sites. Have eating disorders somehow turned into some kind of sick and twisted trend that I didn't know about? If this is the case, I need to say again that there is not enough attention paid to the problem.

I never ever saw my eating disorder as something 'cool' or 'in'; on the contrary, I was extremely embarrassed. Personally, I truly cannot believe that the people responsible for these websites share these sick ideas in order to help others. You do not feel healthy when you have an eating disorder and even though you might get a kick out of losing weight, you still feel weak physically. No one knew, not my mother, not my sister, not my friends, no one. If people today via the internet or another medium are making little clubs to come together in order to kill themselves, the message is clear. They have not the faintest clue as to what they are doing to themselves; and if they do, then they need to seek help, and fast! The severity of the problem cannot be stressed enough.

It breaks my heart to think back at the few times that my mother *did* know about my problem – how it hurt her. My mom worked full-time because my parents divorced when I was thirteen. She would call me several times an hour asking me if I was doing okay and then she would make me swear it. Hearing the impotence in her voice as she asked me those questions made me feel even worse. I always wanted to be the daughter who never gave her problems and now I was keeping her from her work. I was so embarrassed. I cannot imagine the frustration a mother must feel when her child is in such a situation. It must be earth-shattering to know that your daughter or son is depriving him or herself of food and that they are such good actors that you don't know whether to believe what they are saying.

In my case, the divorce had no impact in my life whatsoever. I was the one who encouraged my mother to take the step of divorcing my father. There was never violence or extreme problems at home, but my parents were living as two strangers in the same house. My mother told me one day, 'Darah, the worst loneliness is when you are in the company of another person, and even more so when that person is your husband.' When I heard her talking that way I said, 'Mom, it's time for you to get out! You are still a young woman and you can still start a new life again,' and so she did.

To me every new step or phase in my life was an opportunity to start over again. To end my eating disorder. Every birthday, new house we moved into, Christmas, New Year's eve, or other important dates for that matter, were moments that I really wanted to stop. I would give myself strict deadlines. *After my birthday I will never throw up again* – and then my birthday approached, I would then say, 'What are another few weeks?' No, wait; that's not how it went.

My birthday is December 1st, so I would say to myself that I would have my last big binge on my birthday (because I loved and still do love that Devil's food: cake). But you understand that having a birthday in December meant that Christmas and New Year's were around the corner, and that means more food... To people who don't have an eating disorder, this all sounds ridiculous, but believe me, this is how it goes (or at least for me it did). I couldn't have a small portion of anything, I would have to go all the way. It was all or nothing for me. I could eat practically nothing or if I went over that limit I would have to throw it up again.

It's terrible because, after I got over this problem, I needed to get used to feeling full again. My body would take a really long time to digest what I had eaten, for the simple reason that it didn't need to work for a long time. I gained a few pounds when I started eating normally, but that was such a small price to pay compared to what I felt like again. I could breathe properly; I could finally sleep well again; no more heart palpitations; my skin got healthier; my anxiety attacks were gone, I could concentrate and didn't have this empty and depressed feeling anymore. There are surely many other great things I gained after winning my fight against bulimia, but the best way to describe it is that you just feel good again. You don't live in lies anymore; there is nothing you feel like you need to hide and it feels great! You are no longer lying to anyone, and more importantly, you are no longer lying to yourself, because this is what really destroys you.

After all of this, I can finally enjoy life and food and am able to think about more important things, like what I want to do with my life, my relationship with the most wonderful man on earth and my future husband, Vincent, and the relationship I now have with my mother, which now is more like a solid and special friendship with the woman for whom I have the most admiration. I am surrounded by people who love me (and whom I adore), I am healthy, and more. I have so much to be thankful for. I believe that it is far more important to realise what you have than to be constantly looking for more. I thank God every day for being able to acknowledge all I have been blessed with and more so that I am able to enjoy it.

Five

VINCENT HAS MADE SUCH A DIFFERENCE IN MY LIFE. I am not saying that I was able to overcome my problem because of him, because it just doesn't work that way, but he has really made me realise how great life can really be and I thank him for that.

I met Vincent the first day of freshman year at college. He was sitting in the faculty's canteen (by then he had already graduated) together with two Latin American guys I knew from going out. They quickly introduced me to him, and to be frank, I was so stressed out looking for my class schedule and enrolment forms that I barely remembered how he looked. The only thing that did catch my attention was that he spoke very good Spanish, which impressed me, because during those few seconds one of the other guys explained that Vincent had only been in Buenos Aires, Argentina, for five months.

We would frequently see each other while going out (there are only so many places you can go to in The Hague – it's pretty small). But, you know how it is to talk to people while going out – you say a few inane things, because you just can't get philosophical in a place where you can barely hear 'hello' because the music is so loud. It's hard to communicate after a few drinks on top of the noise, among other things. Another thing that kept me distant was that someone (and I really cannot remember who) told me that he was forty. Now, age is only a number, but at the time I was seventeen, so forty just went too far for me.

Anyway, during one party we managed to talk a bit more and with the help of our hands and feet we were able to tell each other that we liked Motown music. He was impressed that someone my age knew so much about music that was before her time and I really enjoyed talking to him about something I was interested in. At the end of that night he invited me to his birthday, which was the following week, and I accepted. It was then that I understood that he was turning twenty-six (okay, there is still a nine-year difference, but compared to twenty-three, that is nothing).

I thought he was very nice, sociable and good-looking, so I was happy that I had been invited to his birthday. A friend of mine, who was also invited, lived in the same building as he did, which was even better, because this way I was going to be around people I knew.

When I got to the party, he wasn't there. He was throwing his party with two other friends of his. I wasn't feeling very well that night and I wasn't really dressed up for a party either. After about an hour and a half, Vincent finally decided to show up. He quickly said 'hello' and did not bother to speak to me for the rest of the night, because he was under the impression that I was hitting it off with a friend of his (which was absolutely not the case!). All I knew was that I was not getting the attention that I wanted and so I forgot about him as a potential love interest.

But on November 14th, there was a theme party at the faculty's bar and once again, there he was. We started talking and began by exchanging small talk but before we knew it we had been talking for hours on end. During our conversation it suddenly hit me: this was going to be the man that I was going to marry. I don't know where on earth that came from, but I knew it.

At a certain point, they played one of my favourite songs, '*Ojala que llueve café*' by Juan Luis Guerra, and we danced. After that song they played a slower song and that was when he first kissed me. A drunk friend of his tried to be funny by throwing a bucket of cold water over us. I'm talking about November in Holland; it is very cold there during that time of year. After that night, he called my friend for my number and asked me out.

On our first date, it clicked – it was so right. We could not stop talking and he was as engaging as I remembered. I had planned an appointment with another friend three hours after my date with Vincent. I did this because you never know how a date can go and I just wanted to avoid the uncomfortable silences you sometimes get during dates. Although it unfolded to the contrary, perhaps you can understand that, especially for a woman, it is always better to leave too soon than too late. Even though I was struggling with my eating disorder I still had that clear.

During our second date Vincent decided to share some great news, which was that he had finally gotten a job at Amnesty International in Buenos Aires. I couldn't believe it; I was so mad. I didn't know what was worse: that he was leaving or that he sounded so happy that he was leaving. I was furious. After a few more dates I called him and told him that there was no point in seeing each other if he was leaving for six months. He said that he understood, and that was that. I was so angry; how could he understand? Did he not like me? I was disappointed, but I have a theory that it is not worth crying over someone who will not cry over you, so I decided to accept it, hands down.

Let's be honest, we had just met – was I supposed to wait patiently until he decided to come back? I don't think so! Anyway, back then I didn't know him well, so for all I knew he could have very well been the type that chases after everything that moves and cheated on me while in Buenos Aires, then come back and acted as if nothing had ever happened. I wanted to save myself the pain and remain realistic. It is already hard to make a relationship work at long distance, let alone with someone you've only known for a month.

A few days after my phone call to 'call things off' we met again at the same bar where we kissed for the first time. We made some small talk and went back to our friends. I felt him looking at me – you know, that feeling of someone's eyes burning into the back of your head. He walked over, grabbed my hand softly and said, 'I don't want to stop seeing you.' I looked at him and told him that six months was far too long. He said that we could make it work and that he wanted to buy me a ticket to come and visit him after three months to break the time. I still wasn't convinced. I am not a pessimist; I just don't like to get my hopes up when there is a very big chance of them getting crushed. We talked more and before I knew it, we were kissing again.

On December 5th he officially asked me to be his girlfriend and I accepted, although January 9th (the day of his departure) was still haunting me. Three weeks after we were officially a couple, he invited me to Texel (a small Dutch island up in the north) where his parents lived, to celebrate Christmas. I was nervous and honoured at the same time. Christmas went brilliantly; New Year's eve was wonderful; and then came January 8th. I was already sad and when I arrived at his studio, which was completely empty, it was like a sadistic metaphor of how I was feeling. He kept on telling me how bad he felt about leaving, which really annoyed me. 'Why do you feel bad?' I said. 'You are the one who is in control of this situation; I just have to go along with it all. I don't want you to leave and there is nothing I can do to change that, but if you really don't want to leave then you still have a choice.' He just looked at me and said how much he was going to miss me. By this point I was getting angry.

Morning came and I even missed an exam that day to be with him, but I refused to come to the airport. I hate saying goodbye and I was angry at him for making me feel so bad. A group of twenty friends plus family were going to accompany him to the airport and I, his girlfriend, wasn't. The last few minutes before he left we spent together on campus at a café we frequented often. He kept on telling me how sad we looked and my answer was always, 'Don't put us in the same situation, because we are not; *you* are the one who is choosing to leave.' We kissed, hugged and he left.

I felt this nervous, anxious feeling in the pit of my stomach and wondered how on earth I was going to pull it off for six months. A friend of mine was at that café with me for a while and we talked. We then started walking to the bus when my mobile phone rang. It was Said, a friend of Vincent's who told me that he had missed the plane; I was shocked.

After a while, Vincent called me, briefly, because there were no batteries left on his phone. He was ecstatic and yelled, 'Honey, I'm coming back to The Hague; I can't wait to see you!' I was unable to believe my luck. That night, Vincent slept over and decided to go to Argentina for only three weeks – that's a lot better than six months. He already had the ticket and the airline gave him a seat on the next flight the following day. I kissed him goodbye.

While he was in Argentina, we called each other every single day. After a week he called and said that he couldn't wait to see me and that he had bought a ticket for a flight which was leaving in three days. He had bought another ticket for an earlier flight! I felt relieved, because I was missing him so incredibly that whole week. I picked him up at the airport, where we sat for hours laughing at the irony that we call life and how it changes us so dramatically. The six months he was going to leave turned into ten days in only one month.

On March 26th Vincent picked me up late from college with a bag full of stuff. I was so tired that I said that we should go to my mother's house. He kept insisting that it was better to have dinner at my apartment, but I didn't want to.

We ended up going to my mom's. While there, she kept on making comments about him being different than usual (to be honest, this never caught my attention). After an hour or so, he insisted on speaking to me upstairs. We went all the way up to the third floor, which is my mom's room, where he asked me to sit down on the bed. I didn't understand what was going on. He asked me again, until I did. When he got on one knee I realised what he was doing. He asked me to marry him and I immediately said yes.

I was engaged! Barely eighteen and engaged! I couldn't believe it. In Holland this is quite rare; the average age for a woman to get married there is between twenty-eight and thirty years old. We had only been together for three months and three weeks, but it felt right.

On May 25th we celebrated our engagement with a group of friends and family at a beautiful hotel with high tea. I could not have been happier; I was celebrating this blessing that God had granted me and I had the opportunity to share that with my friends and family. In my heart it felt like a miniature wedding. After every glass of champagne, the 'I love you's' were thrown back and forth more and more.

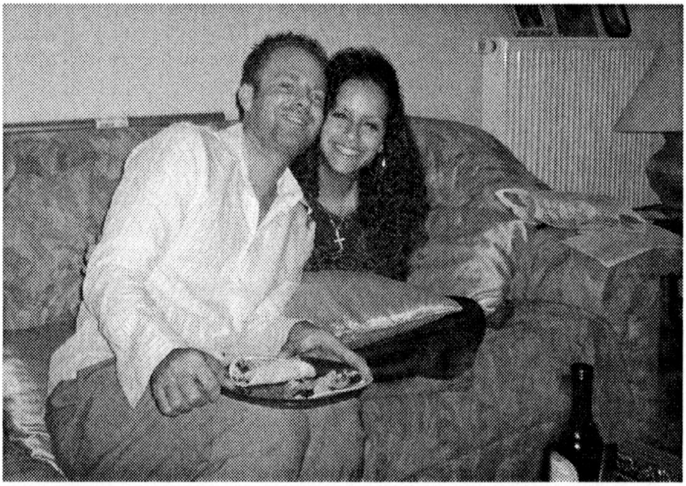

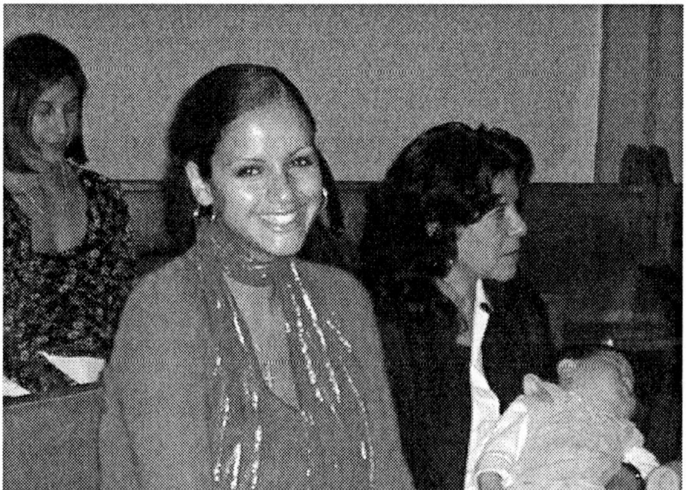

Six

TODAY IS NOVEMBER 13TH, 2003. I AM STILL eighteen for about two more weeks, but God has already given me the greatest gift a woman can ask for. Two days ago I found out that inside of me I was carrying Vincent's child and could hardly believe it. This is something so huge and wonderful that all the money and gold in this world cannot come close to my wealth. I feel so special and honoured to be a channel of life for Vincent and myself and our love for each other. Our love would now be materialised into a little human being, a product of us and our love.

I am about six weeks pregnant and I feel great. I just feel a bit sleepy and have a weird little uncomfortable feeling in my tummy. The baby (if God allows) will be born around the second week of July 2004. I need to make many arrangements for my education, like taking exams for the fourth term in the third, and such. I am determined to complete my Bachelor's in European Studies and, if I am able to, I would like to get a Master's in Latin American Culture. This would have to be evening school, because, to be honest, I really don't feel like studying full-time after my BA anymore. I have a great support system at home. My mother cannot be happier and even my sister bought the first baby clothes and cuddle bunny for the baby. Vincent keeps on saying that he doesn't care what gender the baby is as long as it is healthy (I know secretly he is hoping for a boy).

I am eating healthily now and the days of depriving myself of food seem like centuries ago. Every little thing I eat is to help my baby grow and to make sure I contribute to his or her health to the maximum of my capacity. I am not 'eating for two', but I do eat healthily. My body now has another function, which is to be the home for my baby for nine months and nothing else. I love this baby so much already and the more I think about it, the more I love it and the bigger this miracle is to me. Vincent and I already have names, but I cannot disclose them.

These two days have been incredible; I cannot wait to find out what gender the baby is. Once I know, I will probably be anxious to know how the baby looks. I know many people around me who think that I should not be having a baby this young, but I don't care. I am responsible; I have already started saving money for the baby before I knew I was pregnant and I have experience working with children as I have worked in day-care centres on and off for two years now. I am not saying that I know all there is to know about babies, but at least I am not completely in the dark about it.

There will never be the 'perfect time' for a baby, but one thing I can guarantee is that no other baby on this earth will receive more love or a warmer welcome than this little one!

I do not believe that my case can be compared to that of the average pregnant teen. I have completed high school and have the support of my family, which is more important than anything else. I feel privileged to be able to celebrate and enjoy this phase of my life instead of having to be ashamed or scared. My heart goes out to those girls who are faced with problems in their family caused by something that should be seen for what it is – a tremendously beautiful gift from heaven.

People will always talk, especially when they can be distracted that way from having to be confronted with their own life. I am not on earth to please others. I live and let live; that which is said about me which cannot contribute to my life in a positive way can be forgotten. I used to be very much preoccupied with other people's opinion of me; why? There are so many people and each and every one of them has their own opinion, so I will never ever be able to please them all. So why bother? At the end of the day I go to bed with all my actions on my conscience and at that moment I am alone. All those people who were dying to complain about my ways are gone, and I am confronted only with myself.

Even if I had done everything in my power to please all these people, the one and only person I would have to contend with at the end of the day would be myself.

You can live your whole life trying to make others happy and making sure that no one has a bad thing to say about you till the day you die, but I don't choose that route. The day I die I will look back and remember all I have done during my time on earth and whether these things were right or wrong will not matter, because the only one I can blame or congratulate is myself, and no one else.

This might bring me to harder places, but I will be

able to stand up, take charge and acknowledge that I was able to think and make decisions for myself. That alone will give me far greater satisfaction than any other thing and the same goes for you.

Since I was five my dream had always been being an actress. I had an incredible fascination for the art of drama. The Oscars were a greatly celebrated event at home and I remember praying to God each night in bed for an opportunity to be present at the Oscars one day. I would stand in front of the mirror pretending to have an interview with Oprah Winfrey about my latest movie and the thought that this dream could one day come true worked as a huge motivation for me. Years later, after many, many photo shoots and auditions, I got a call from a casting agency in Amsterdam. They had gotten my photos from another casting agency that had closed and had put all their clients' photos on the web. They asked me to come to Amsterdam to audition for a duo, which involved both dancing and acting, I couldn't believe it! I could finally see my dream becoming real.

I was very nervous for the audition, but I gave my all. I was asked to come back for the second round. This time I was more confident and I got the part. During the third visit, it started – I had to lose weight. I'm not mad at the agency, because they just had to deliver a certain package that the producers wanted to see, but still. I would get called several times a week to be asked whether I had lost the weight and whether I was exercising enough. Needless to say, it was hardcore bulimia at that time. I was obsessed with losing weight (which I of course already was); the only thing this time was that I had a deadline.

Don't think I was overweight; I was a normal girl with Latin curves. They had a more athletic-type body in mind, which makes me giggle now, because that was just not me. On the other hand I was watching TV the other day and heard model Heidi Klum being described as 'curvy'. What? The woman has a good body, but come on! If *that* is curvaceous these days, then I really need to get the Marilyn Monroe-type figure out of my head. No wonder; if *that's* curvy, then yeah, I am definitely fat.

I felt so much pressure at this point that I ate more and threw up more to compensate. Only, I wasn't losing any weight and knew that the agency was not going to be happy.

I was very frustrated, because back then I blamed myself. I was convinced that they were right; they should know what beauty was, they were in the 'beauty business' for crying out loud. I was just too fat. Instead of feeling good about myself I felt worse than ever before. My mother soon suspected that something was wrong and advised me to call it quits and I did. Shortly after, I felt regret, but now I am happy to not have conformed to the idiotic image of beauty that the media propagates these days. It is not only perverse but also irresponsible; you could even go so far as to call it *fatal*.

Seven

AT A CERTAIN POINT IT JUST NEEDS TO STOP. THERE just comes a point when you need to wake up and realise the damage that you are causing and that needs to be the end. I believe that everyone who is harming him or herself through an eating disorder, by drinking too much or even by using drugs, realises at a certain point what is going on. I am convinced that this 'point' is crucial, because it is then that you can no longer claim to 'not be aware'. This will be your greatest opportunity to get out. The fall this time is even harder than the times before when you 'tried' to quit. I write 'tried' in quotation marks because I truly believe that everyone can succeed when they really try and when they don't is when they fall off the wagon and go wrong. It might sound harsh, but it helped me.

Think about what thought can motivate you most, the thought that you had which pushed you to give your all in fighting whatever it was that you were fighting. Do not lose perspective of what is going on, that is all. You should be aware that your eating disorder is killing you – that is a fact. But this does not mean that the solution is going to be as hard or difficult because of the severity of the problem. People usually assume that big problems are always immediately linked to very difficult or impossible solutions, when the only thing making the solution impossible is that very thought. Bulimia to me was a lifestyle, no longer a dangerous habit, and all it took for me to break the only pattern I knew for nine years was the right mentality, the thought that stopping was really not as hard as I thought.

The feeling of being 'full' after eating had become practically unknown to me. I had to wait for my stomach to digest my food before I felt full for a few minutes till I went to the bathroom. And after half an hour I would be hungry again.

Life is all about changes and adapting to the new situation. My mother would always tell me '*El ser humano es un animal de cambio*' which means, 'Human beings are animals of change' and no thing or being is able to adapt as well as we can. Just make sure that the change or new situation is of a positive and beneficial nature.

You know what is good for you and what you need to do to get out of a bad situation better than anyone else. You can fool the world, but you can't fool yourself. If you feel you have read many clichés in this book, maybe the reason why a cliché becomes a cliché is because it is an accumulation of similar experiences by many different people. It is universal advice built upon a shared feeling. Do what you feel is necessary to help yourself; talk to that person with whom you feel you connect and who touches you. Any habit or addiction is in your control; sometimes it's just easier to think that there is some greater power controlling it, when that greater power is actually only yourself. That is the only thing you need to know in order to defeat your problem.

Good luck and God bless.

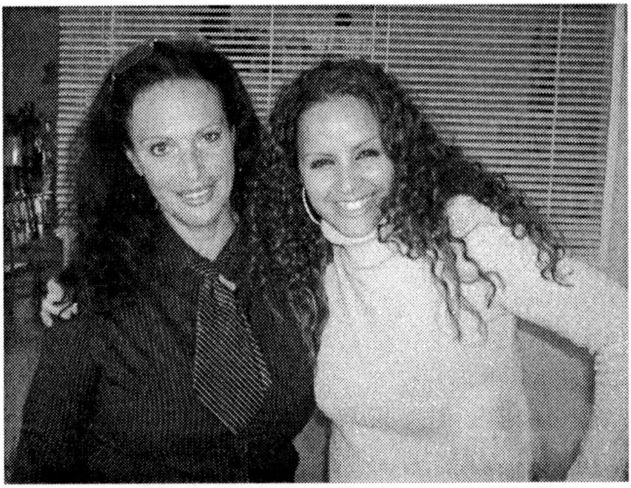

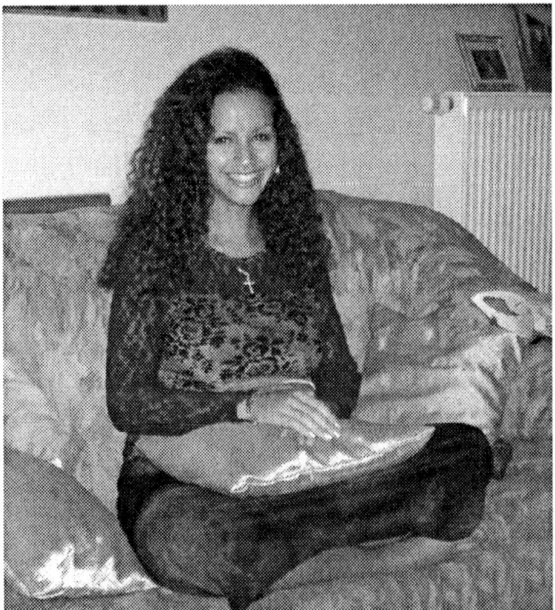

Pages out of my diary

December 1st, 1998

My birthday is today and I am sure that after today I will look back and think, *The day after my 14th birthday was the day I stopped throwing up*. I can't stop today, it's just too hard because there's going to be all this food and stuff. Today is the last day I throw up – really!

   0 calories till now, haven't started my day yet.
   Weighing 65.5 kg (133 lbs)

December 2nd, 1998

I knew that I wouldn't be able to make it! I just came back from the bathroom; I am so stupid! I hadn't eaten much and wanted to go to bed hungry, because when I go to bed hungry I always lose weight, but I couldn't. My mom came home with nice things from the store and I couldn't stay away, why am I so weak?

   ? calories
   Weighing 65.5 kg

December 3rd, 1998

I was thinking that there is not much use trying to quit throwing up now, because the month December is just too hard. First, my birthday on the first, the *Sinterklaas* (Dutch National holiday) on the fifth, then Christmas and New Year's eve! I might as well wait until the New Year – what better way to start the last year of the millennium?

December 4th, 1998

I threw up so much yesterday that my throat was sore and hurting this morning. I was also really thirsty and my hands and feet were really swollen. I think I have lost weight, but I do feel sick. It's just these last days before the New Year and after that I will just watch my weight and lose it the normal and healthy way.

I was at a friend's house yesterday and I was so jealous because she could enjoy the food. She wasn't anxious to go and throw it up; food wasn't an issue and that made me wonder whether food could ever not be an issue for me? I feel like such a liar, hiding everything from my mom and I pray to God that He forgives me for all those times that I swore to her that I was okay (about not throwing up) when I wasn't. I guess God understands that I lie because I want to protect her. She's just so worried about Valeria these days that I don't want to worry her even more, because I can make it on my own.

? calories (I'm not sure what stayed in)
64.5 kg

January 1st, 1999

I threw up last night, but does that count? I mean it was the 31st still, and okay, the first 'officially' starts at twelve, but everyone goes to bed and wakes up thinking that it's a new day anyway, right? Why shouldn't it apply to me then?

I haven't eaten anything yet and I think that if I follow the schedule below, I will be able to not throw up and lose weight at the same time.

Breakfast
Coffee with saccharin (0 cal)
2 apples (120 cal)

Lunch
2 apples (120 cal)
4 crackers (160 cal)

Dinner
Instant tomato soup (50 cal)
4 crackers (160 cal)

Total = 610 cal + a lot of water!
Weighing 65 kg

January 2nd, 1999

I did it! I lost another kilo (more or less 2 lbs); I feel lighter! It took me a while to sleep, because I was so hungry, but I lost the kilo!

Weighing 64 kg!

★

March 15th, 1999

I threw up again. I feel so empty, but even more alone than anything else. I don't know why; it wasn't even for really good food – I just started eating a sandwich and then another and by the third, I felt so stupid for doing it that I ate a fourth, drank chocolate milk and threw it up again. By the time I realised what I had done I already heard the toilet flushing and felt the blood going to my head.

If I make sure that it only sticks to this one day, then it's not that bad I think.

? calories
64 kg

March 16th, 1999

I'm not sure whether I will succeed not throwing up again today, because I'm eating at a friend's house. I should have said no! I'm not ready for this kind of stuff yet!

I f**king gained half a kilo back! I am so angry, I don't want to go anywhere; I'm going to cancel later on, because I know I won't be able to keep it in. I've been cancelling appointments a lot lately; I just want to be thin for once in my life! Once I'm thin I can lead a normal life, I know it.

0 calories (just woke up)
64.5 kg

March 17th, 1999

I did it again – I threw up. If I just make sure that the relapse is only three days and not more, then I have until tomorrow to get my act together again. It's so frustrating. Why can't I get rid of this problem? I managed to control it for about three months and still it is as if it still controls me. When will that power over me stop?

I am killing myself, I know. Only after two days I am already feeling the damage. It might sound stupid, but after those three months I forgot the side effects of bulimia. Bulimia… I'm bulimic, I can't believe it. I knew that I had a problem for a long time, but seeing that word on paper now is making me realise what is going on, I am bulimic. You hear about eating disorders, but somehow you feel that what you have is different. I feel so trapped and feel as if food will never be a normal part of my life; what should I do? Nobody knows I still have it. The people who know about this problem think that it is a thing of the past. I hope that one day I will really talk of this problem as something of the past without knowing better.

64 kg

March 18th, 1999

I have nothing to say anymore, I guess I should accept that this is a problem which I shall take to my grave. There is just no way out. The days that I don't throw up are such a struggle and sooner or later things will go wrong anyway and I end up falling off the wagon. What I said yesterday was true: I feel the damage that I am causing to my body and the scary part is that this is apparently not enough motivation for me to stop.

Sometimes I forget why I even throw up. Before, I used to know the reason – because I wanted to lose weight. Nowadays it feels more like a habit. Even if I did stop those three months, falling back into this routine feels oddly familiar to me. I actually cannot remember a time anymore when this was not a problem in my life and that makes me really sad. I wish I could find help or knew at least what to do. The last time my mom found out it made her really sad and I don't want to make her go through that again. A factor which also plays part in the reason why I don't tell my mom is because I feel ashamed of being this weak. If I were strong I wouldn't have fallen back; if I were strong I wouldn't be in this mess, period.

63.5 kg
? calories

May 5th, 1999

This summer my mom, my sister and I are going to visit friends who live in Cyprus, and after, I'm going to Menorca (a Spanish island). I can't wait. I have about a month; the time to lose more weight – I need to look good in my bathing suit. I hope that this time I can finally meet my deadline. I am so sick of making these plans and not pulling through, this time has to be different!

63.5 kg

May 6th, 1999

I have made a food schedule for this coming month, which I will have to follow very carefully. It's made up out of a week plan.

Monday
Breakfast: 2 apples + coffee = 120 cal
Lunch: 1 apple + 2 crackers + water = 120 cal
Dinner: soluble soup + 2 crackers + water = 90 cal
Total = 330 cal

Tuesday
Breakfast: 1 glass of milk + apple = 120 cal
Lunch: 1 slice of bread + water = 100 cal
Dinner: soluble soup + 2 crackers + water = 90 cal
Total = 310 cal

Wednesday
Breakfast: 1 glass of juice + 1 apple = 120 cal
Lunch: 2 crackers + 1 banana = 170 cal
Dinner: 2 apples = 120 cal
Total = 410 cal

Thursday
Breakfast: 1 glass of milk + 2 crackers = 110 cal
Lunch: soluble soup + 2 apples = 160 cal
Dinner: 1 glass of milk + 2 crackers = 110 cal
Total = 380 cal

Friday
Breakfast = coffee + juice + banana = 180 cal
Lunch. = 3 crackers + water = 75 cal
Dinner = 2 apples + tea = 120 cal
Total = 375 cal

Saturday
Breakfast: coffee + 1 apple = 60 cal
Lunch: yoghurt = 120 cal
Dinner: soluble soup = 40 cal
Total = 220 cal

Sunday
Breakfast: coffee + yoghurt = 120 cal
Lunch: 2 crackers + juice = 110 cal
Dinner: 2 apples = 120 cal
Total = 350 cal

August 3rd, 1999

I haven't written anything for so long, because I was on vacation. Cyprus was great. Unfortunately I did throw up and felt like a complete loser. In Menorca I didn't come out during the day; I was too ashamed to wear a bathing suit. The only thing I did during the day was sit inside the apartment and smoke my dad's cigarettes. I failed again; I hate it. Another summer without me reaching my goal, but hey, there's nothing new about that.

August 15th, 1999

I thought that I was going to die last night, what am I doing to myself? I woke up sweating like hell while I had this immense fear of something, which I cannot place. I prayed to God to get me through the night, because I felt as if wasn't going to make it. My heart was going crazy and my mouth was dry. When I tried walking to the toilet I was shaking uncontrollably. I cannot remember ever being that scared. I really need to get my sh*t together, because I know that I will not make it to see twenty-five if I go on like this. I feel my body's damage with every single breath that I take. I can't breathe properly anymore and at night I always need to sit up straight as a candle, in order to get enough oxygen in. I need to get out of this hell, I can't take this pain anymore. IT HAS TO STOP!

God, please help me! Give me the strength and the will to live, because I know this is going to be my death.

August 23rd, 1999

Sometimes I wonder what would happen if I just gave up and accept that Bulimia is just a part of me? The girls I see on TV have only had the problem for a little while, when in my situation we are talking about a lifestyle. I cannot imagine a life without me worrying about my weight, it seems too far away.

Would it really kill me? It is not that I do not want to stop, it is just that it feels so impossible and hard to do. I wish I could wake up from this dream and go on living a life in which my weight, nor the calories that I have consumed play the leading role. Maybe the damage is just too great.

63 kg

August 24th, 1999

I feel so sad. I cannot explain it. I just feel numb and fake. I hate having to lie; I hate having to fake being this person who I am not. Someone described me as being confident the other day – yeah right. I cannot even take pride in that, because I am not confident, I am by far the weakest person I know and every virtue people give me credit for is just another thing in which I cannot take pride, because it is not me.

I have convinced everyone around me that I am the person that I am not, the only person I need to convince and change is myself. It is just so hard to be proud of myself when I cannot even be in control of something so stupid as throwing up! What kind of problem is this? The thought of throwing up being a problem in my life embarrasses me. For heaven's sake, there are people starving, in war and this is my problem? I am so angry at myself, what is my problem?

August 28th, 1999

I am not even going to register when I throw up or not anymore, there is just no point in doing that. I am weak and stupid and I have accepted that. Every time that I look in the mirror after having thrown up I feel such a rage towards myself. God give me the enlightenment to stop this stupidity, I want to live again and this is no longer a life.

September 11th, 1999

I have not thrown up for eight days and I feel a lot better. I can breathe normally and I feel more focused. I am still weighing 63 kg and I am just trying not to feel full, because I know that is when I feel tempted to throw up. I hope this time it is final and that throwing up will be something of the past. It is so frustrating to me, because I have said and felt this before. I wish that I had some kind of guarantee that this time will last.

September 15th, 1999

I cannot believe it. I threw up again, but that is not all. A few nights ago there was this movie on TV about a bulimic/anorexic woman and it made me feel so guilty and ashamed. I felt pity for her and when I realised that I was in the same situation, I felt the same for myself. This whole situation is so damn pathetic. Is that really how I would look to a stranger who looked into my life? God help me, please.

September 23rd, 1999

I keep on getting these wounds on my face, which take weeks to heal. They start out as a blemish and when I scratch at them (only for a bit) they turn into these big wounds that look like burn marks. Could this have to do with the fact that I throw up? It could also be hormones, I guess.

October 4th, 1999

Last week I went out and got really drunk. I locked myself up in the bathroom and stared at myself in the mirror for what felt like hours. I saw myself and asked the person staring back at me in the mirror what was wrong with me. I started crying and thought, when is this pain finally going to stop tormenting me from inside?

October 7th, 1999

I wonder what people around me would think if they knew what I was going through? Would they treat me as a weak person, would they admire my honesty? It makes me think, because I know that many people would not be able to believe it. I do not know; this whole situation is just linked to weakness and helplessness and I do not want anyone to pity me, or feel sorry for me for that matter.

62.5 kg

★

December 9th, 2003

Reading all those old pages of my diary from the time that I was going through all those hard moments feels like the monster in your room which you would ask your mother to scare away. I cannot process how bulimia at a certain point in my life *was* my life and how it now is but a vague memory together with all the rest. It is not that it no longer crosses my mind – it does, but it is more that I think back on those times as a personal victory. I cannot believe that this page is meant to end up in my book! My book, for crying out loud!

Here I am, the same girl who had accepted eating disorders to be a part of her, now writing a book for others in that very situation. I hope it makes a difference because I do believe that eating disorders can one day be these 'weird things' that people used to have in the past.

Today I am in my second year of college, engaged, healthy and most important of all, pregnant. Life is indeed all about changes and whether these are positive or negative is all up to us, and to be honest that to me is a comforting thought.

Calories today = ?
Kg = who cares!

A Few More Things…

I HOPE THAT THIS BOOK HAS BEEN SOME FORM OF help to you, not to mention proof that you can overcome an eating disorder. Remember, never consider yourself 'a victim', because at that moment you are surrendering yourself to the problem, when actually, you are the only one in this situation who is in control. The people around you who love you are the victims, because they can't control your mind, but you can. They suffer together with you. I wrote this book because in my heart I felt that reading this, coming from someone my age, could have been the little push in the right direction that I truly needed then.

No matter how dark your world seems now and how wrapped up in your secrets you feel – even to this there is an end and a solution and the only one who can end the pain is you. Like I have written in other parts of this book, I thought that I had to accept myself as a bulimic for the rest of my life, thank God that I did not. There is nothing that controls you, there is no greater power, such as bulimia or anorexia – that thought only makes you weak, when you are not. This problem can be fatal and so is not at all a light matter, but this does not mean that the solution to this problem is accordingly hard. Seeking help is also the key – whether it is your mother, or that study hall supervisor that looks so compassionate. Like I wrote before, the only thing you need is the will to live and if you have that, then you have found your solution.

Facing the Facts

IN ORDER TO SAVE YOU TIME I'VE DONE SOME research on anorexia and bulimia. There is of course a lot more information on this topic, but I wanted to keep this book more in the theme of my experience and personal view on bulimia and anorexia. On the web or in the library you can find a lot of information written by doctors on the physical damage caused by these two problems.

The following information is based on medical facts, so if you're still not sure whether you or someone you know suffers from a disorder, then here are some points to clear up your suspicions:

SYMPTOMS OF ANOREXIA

1. Intense fear of eating
2. Excessive exercising
3. Obsession about food and calories
4. Wanting to lose weight when normal weight or underweight
5. Always feeling cold
6. Moodiness and sleeping problems
7. Increasing isolation and loss of friends
8. Wearing baggy clothes to disguise weight loss
9. Reluctance to admit to having a problem
10. Reduced libido (less need for sexual contact)
11. Fainting and dizzy spells
12. Growth of downy hair all over the body

SYMPTOMS OF BULIMIA:
1. Consuming enormous numbers of calories at one sitting
2. Disappearing to the toilet after food is consumed to vomit
3. Secretive behaviour, mood swings
4. Feeling out of control, helpless and lonely
5. No energy, generally unwell
6. Sore throat
7. Digestive problems
8. Erosion of teeth enamel, caused by vomiting stomach acids
9. Salivary enlargement in cheeks
10. Poor skin condition
11. Dehydration
12. Reluctance to admit to having a problem

No other disorder has a higher death rate than eating disorders. If you find that you have several of the symptoms mentioned above please seek help as fast as possible. Eating disorders are seen as *fatal psychological diseases!*[4]

---

[4] All the information mentioned above was found on the following website: www.eatingdisorderscentre.co.uk

Printed in the United Kingdom
by Lightning Source UK Ltd.
120458UK00001B/98